HEAVEN ON EARTH
101 Happy Poems

Edited by
WENDY COPE

faber and faber

First published in 2001
by Faber and Faber Limited
Bloomsbury House
74–77 Great Russell Street
London WC1B 3DA

Photoset by Wilmaset Ltd, Wirral
Printed in England by TJ International Ltd, Padstow, Cornwall

A CIP record for this book
is available from the British Library

ISBN 978-0-571-20706-0

8 10 9 7

Contents

Introduction

'Happiness writes white.' I am reliably informed that it was the French novelist Henri de Montherlant who first made this statement, presumably in French. While I've been working on this anthology, I've come across a similar opinion in the work of several poets. Hans Magnus Enzensberger, in a poem entitled 'Joy', writes 'she does not want me to speak of her/ she won't be put down on paper' (English translation by Michael Hamburger). The late Gavin Ewart, a writer for whom I have the greatest respect, took the view that 'Happiness is the one emotion a poem can't capture.' And D. J. Enright, another poet whose work I admire, penned these lines: 'The happiness you must take as read,/ The writing of it is so difficult.' Difficult but not impossible. There is one little poem by Enright in this book, and one by Gavin as well.

Each of these writers may have been speaking just for himself, rather than making a generalisation about literature. But 'Happiness writes white' seems to be accepted as a self-evident and universal truth by a surprising number of other writers – I wish I had a pound for every time I've seen it quoted approvingly in a book review.

I use the word 'surprising' because one doesn't have to think very hard or be very widely read to see that it isn't always true. What is the best-known poem in the English language? Probably the one by Wordsworth which ends 'And then my heart with pleasure fills,/ And dances with the daffodils.' And what is the feeling in those lines? Yes, some readers will say, it *is* happy, but it is a thoroughly irritating poem and I've hated it since my schooldays. I didn't like it either, when I was at school, but I changed my mind and I urge those readers to give it another chance. If you still think the poem we know as 'Daffodils' is lousy, then read the other 100. If you don't find anything that is both (a) convincingly happy and (b) a good poem, then I have lost the argument.

It is more than ten years since, tired of merely shaking my head and muttering 'Rubbish!', I decided to compile an anthology of happy poems. I began to make a note whenever I happened to come across one. Many of my books now have an 'H' pencilled on the fly leaf, followed by a list of page numbers. I would have liked to continue working on the project in an intermittent and leisurely fashion for another twenty years but I was afraid that someone else would have the same idea and rush into print with it. So I agreed a deadline with Faber, and have spent the last four months reading books of poems, looking for the happy ones.

It's been wonderful and I'm sorry it's over. The great thing about editing an anthology is that you are paid to read. I've plugged some of the more embarrassing gaps in my knowledge of English poetry and made many exciting discoveries – not all of them happy poems, because I was very willing to be sidetracked. Happiness, as I already knew, writes much less than misery. However, I never doubted that I would be able to find the 101 I needed for this book. In my file there are 167 others that didn't make it into the final selection.

At quite a late stage, when I told a few people what I was working on, their reactions were interesting. Several, of course, thought it would be very, very difficult, if not impossible, to produce such a book. One friend, who didn't consider the job impossible, asked 'But won't they all be about love?' A lot of them are about love – of lovers, spouses, children. There are also poems about places, the beauty of the natural world and the changing seasons, about company and solitude, about music, books, food and drink, and the pleasure of taking a shower. And there are some religious poems. And, yes, you could, broadly, say that they are all about love.

More than one person asked if the poems would all be funny. Now, that *would* have been a difficult job. In my introduction to an earlier anthology, *The Funny Side*, I pointed out that quite a few of the poems arose from despair and misery. Life can seem so terrible that the only possible response is laughter. 'Happiness', says Bishop Whately in his *Apophthegms*, is 'no laughing matter'. Up to a point, my lord. We can laugh just because we're so happy, as Fleur Adcock does in the first poem in this book. And there is some humour in a few of the poems but I wouldn't include any of them in an anthology of comic verse.

Some of them bring a broad smile to my face. Others bring tears to my eyes. Though the book sprang, as I have said, from the wish to prove a point, it became more than that, as I found myself absorbed in the attempt to create a celebration of those moments of happiness that most of us do, in spite of everything, experience.

My thanks to Paul Keegan, poetry editor at Faber, and to Angela Baker, Sheila Burns, Jane Feaver, Greg Gatenby, Dave Gelly, Adèle Geras, Becci Lynch, Mark Oakley, Suzi Rae, Kit Wright and Rob Wyke, all of whom have suggested poems, lent me books, or helped in other ways. Thanks, too, to the staffs of the South Bank Poetry Library and Moberly Library at Winchester College. And special thanks to Lachlan Mackinnon, who has been very generous with his

time, and whose knowledge, critical acumen and extensive
collection of poetry books have all been valuable resources.

WENDY COPE
October 2000

HEAVEN ON EARTH

Londoner

Scarcely two hours back in the country
and I'm shopping in East Finchley High Road
in a cotton skirt, a cardigan, jandals –
or flipflops as people call them here,
where February's winter. Aren't I cold?
The neighbours in their overcoats are smiling
at my smiles and not at my bare toes:
they know me here.
              I hardly know myself,
yet. It takes me until Monday evening,
walking from the office after dark
to Westminster Bridge. It's cold, it's foggy,
the traffic's as abominable as ever,
and there across the Thames is County Hall,
that uninspired stone body, floodlit.
It makes me laugh. In fact, it makes me sing.

Ode

The spacious firmament on high,
With all the blue ethereal sky,
And spangled heav'ns, a shining frame,
Their great original proclaim:
Th' unwearied sun, from day to day,
Does his Creator's power display,
And publishes to every land
The work of an almighty hand.

Soon as the evening shades prevail,
The moon takes up the wondrous tale,
And nightly to the list'ning earth
Repeats the story of her birth:
Whilst all the stars that round her burn,
And all the planets in their turn,
Confirm the tidings as they roll,
And spread the truth from pole to pole.

What though, in solemn silence, all
Move round the dark terrestrial ball?
What though nor real voice nor sound
Amid their radiant orbs be found?
In reason's ear they all rejoice,
And utter forth a glorious voice,
For ever singing, as they shine,
'The hand that made us is divine.'

Poems of Solitary Delights

What a delight it is
When on the bamboo matting
In my grass-thatched hut,
All on my own,
I make myself at ease.

What a delight it is
When, borrowing
Rare writings from a friend,
I open out
The first sheet.

What a delight it is
When, spreading paper,
I take my brush
And find my hand
Better than I thought.

What a delight it is
When, after a hundred days
Of racking my brains,
That verse that wouldn't come
Suddenly turns out well.

What a delight it is
When, of a morning,
I get up and go out
To find in full bloom a flower
That yesterday was not there.

What a delight it is
When, skimming through the pages

Of a book, I discover
A man written of there
Who is just like me.

What a delight it is
When everyone admits
It's a very difficult book,
And I understand it
With no trouble at all.

What a delight it is
When I blow away the ash,
To watch the crimson
Of the glowing fire
And hear the water boil.

What a delight it is
When a guest you cannot stand
Arrives, then says to you
'I'm afraid I can't stay long,'
And soon goes home.

What a delight it is
When I find a good brush,
Steep it hard in water,
Lick it on my tongue
And give it its first try.

ANONYMOUS

Pangur Bán

*Written by a student of the monastery of Carinthia on a copy of
St Paul's Epistles, in the eighth century*

I and Pangur Bán, my cat,
'Tis a like task we are at;
Hunting mice is his delight,
Hunting words I sit all night.

Better far than praise of men
'Tis to sit with book and pen;
Pangur bears me no ill-will,
He too plies his simple skill.

'Tis a merry thing to see
At our tasks how glad are we,
When at home we sit and find
Entertainment to our mind.

Oftentimes a mouse will stray
In the hero Pangur's way;
Oftentimes my keen thought set
Takes a meaning in its net.

'Gainst the wall he sets his eye
Full and fierce and sharp and sly;
'Gainst the wall of knowledge I
All my little wisdom try.

When a mouse darts from its den,
O how glad is Pangur then!
O what gladness do I prove
When I solve the doubts I love!

So in peace our tasks we ply,
Pangur Bán, my cat, and I;
In our arts we find our bliss,
I have mine and he has his.

Practice every day has made
Pangur perfect in his trade;
I get wisdom day and night
Turning darkness into light.

Translated from the Gaelic by Robin Flower

Sumer is icumen in,
Loud sing cuckoo!
Groweth seed and bloweth mead
And springeth the wood now.
Sing cuckoo!

Ewe bleateth after lamb,
Cow loweth after calf,
Bullock starteth, buck farteth,
Merry sing cuckoo!

Cuckoo, cuckoo!
Well singest thou cuckoo,
Nor cease thou never now!

Sing cuckoo now, sing cuckoo!
Sing cuckoo, sing cuckoo now!

The Catch

Forget
the long, smouldering
afternoon. It is

this moment
when the ball scoots
off the edge

of the bat; upwards,
backwards, falling
seemingly

beyond him
yet he reaches
and picks it

out
of its loop
like

an apple
from a branch,
the first of the season.

Calypso

Dríver drive fáster and máke a good rún
Down the Springfield Line únder the shíning sún.

Flý like an aéroplane, dón't pull up shórt
Till you bráke for Grand Céntral Státion, New Yórk.

For thére in the míddle of thát waiting-háll
Should be stánding the óne that Í love best of áll.

If he's nót there to méet me when Í get to tówn,
I'll stánd on the síde-walk with téars rolling dówn.

For hé is the óne that I lóve to look ón,
The ácme of kíndness and pérfectión.

He présses my hánd and he sáys he loves mé,
Which I fínd an admiráble pecúliaritý.

The wóods are bright gréen on both sídes of the líne;
The trées have their lóves though they're dífferent from
     míne.

But the póor fat old bánker in the sún-parlor cár
Has nó one to lóve him excépt his cigár.

If Í were the Héad of the Chúrch or the Státe,
I'd pówder my nóse and just téll them to wáit.

For lóve's more impórtant and pówerful thán
Éven a príest or a pólit…

My Orcha'd in Linden Lea

'Ithin the woodlands, flow'ry gleäded,
  By the woak tree's mossy moot,
The sheenen grass-bleädes, timber-sheäded,
  Now do quiver under voot;
An' birds do whissle over head,
An' water's bubblen in its bed,
An' there vor me the apple tree
Do leän down low in Linden Lea.

When leaves that leätely wer a-springen
  Now do feäde 'ithin the copse,
An' païnted birds do hush their zingen
  Up upon the timber's tops;
An' brown-leav'd fruit's a-turnen red,
In cloudless zunsheen, over head,
Wi' fruit vor me, the apple tree
Do leän down low in Linden Lea.

Let other vo'k meäke money vaster
  In the aïr o' dark-room'd towns,
I don't dread a peevish meäster;
  Though noo man do heed my frowns,
I be free to goo abrode,
Or teäke ageän my homeward road
To where, vor me, the apple tree
Do leän down low in Linden Lea.

Soothsayer

I'm sure you will be very happy with this bra, Madam,
she said, her manicure seriously red as she tapped the till.
Of course I did not ask her how she knew.

Who is rude enough to challenge the clairvoyant,
the diagnostician, the prognosticator?
But she was right. As soon as she folded up

the lacy garment – its ticket swinging insouciantly –
and handed it across the counter
in its raspberry-pink bag, my spirits rose.

Outside, traffic parted for me like the Red Sea:
the sun appeared and gilded passers-by
who nervously returned my random smiles.

The days, the weeks, wore on in a numinous haze
of goodwill. Who knows why? Be cynical if you must:
I only record the sequence of events.

Seaside Golf

How straight it flew, how long it flew,
   It clear'd the rutty track
And soaring, disappeared from view
   Beyond the bunker's back –
A glorious, sailing, bounding drive
That made me glad I was alive.

And down the fairway, far along
   It glowed a lonely white;
I played an iron sure and strong
   And clipp'd it out of sight,
And spite of grassy banks between
I knew I'd find it on the green.

And so I did. It lay content
   Two paces from the pin;
A steady putt and then it went
   Oh, most securely in.
The very turf rejoiced to see
That quite unprecedented three.

Ah! seaweed smells from sandy caves
   And thyme and mist in whiffs,
In-coming tide, Atlantic waves
   Slapping the sunny cliffs,
Lark song and sea sounds in the air
And splendour, splendour everywhere.

To my Dear and Loving Husband

If ever two were one, then surely we.
If ever man were loved by wife, then thee;
If ever wife was happy in a man,
Compare with me, ye women, if you can.
I prize thy love more than whole mines of gold
Or all the riches that the East doth hold.
My love is such that rivers cannot quench,
Nor ought but love from thee, give recompense.
Thy love is such I can no way repay,
The heavens reward thee manifold, I pray.
Then while we live, in love let's so persevere
That when we live no more, we may live ever.

Meeting at Night

The grey sea and the long black land;
And the yellow half-moon large and low;
And the startled little waves that leap
In fiery ringlets from their sleep,
As I gain the cove with pushing prow,
And quench its speed i' the slushy sand.

Then a mile of warm sea-scented beach;
Three fields to cross till a farm appears;
A tap at the pane, the quick sharp scratch
And blue spurt of a lighted match,
And a voice less loud, thro' its joys and fears,
Than the two hearts beating each to each!

A Poet's Welcome to his love-begotten Daughter; the first instance that entitled him to the venerable appellation of Father

Thou's welcome, wean! Mischanter fa' me,
If thoughts o' thee, or yet thy Mamie,
Shall ever daunton me or awe me,
  My bonie lady;
Or if I blush when thou shalt ca' me
  Tyta, or Daddie.

Though now they ca' me fornicator,
And tease my name in kintra clatter,
The mair they talk, I'm kend the better;
  E'en let them clash!
An auld wife's tongue's a feckless matter
  To gie ane fash.

Welcome! My bonie, sweet, wee dochter!
Though ye come here a wee unsought for;
And though your comin I hae fought for,
  Baith Kirk and Queir;
Yet by my faith, ye're no unwrought for,
  That I shall swear!

Wee image o' my bonie Betty,
As fatherly I kiss and daut thee,
As dear and near my heart I set thee,
  Wi' as gude will,
As a' the Priests had seen me get thee
  That's out o' h—.

Sweet fruit o' monie a merry dint,
My funny toil is no a' tint;
Though ye come to the warld asklent,
	Which fools may scoff at,
In my last plack your part's be in't,
	The better half o't.

Though I should be the waur bestead,
Thou 's be as braw and bienly clad,
And thy young years as nicely bred
	Wi' education,
As any brat o' Wedlock's bed,
	In a' thy station.

Lord grant that thou may ay inherit
Thy Mither's looks an' gracefu' merit;
An' thy poor, worthless Daddie's spirit,
	Without his failins!
'Twad please me mair to see thee heir it
	Than stocked mailins!

For if thou be, what I wad hae thee,
And tak the counsel I shall gie thee,
I'll never rue my trouble wi' thee,
	The cost nor shame o't,
But be a loving Father to thee,
	And brag the name o't.

wean, child; *Mischanter*, mishap; *daunton*, subdue; *Tyta*, pet name for father; *kintra clatter*, country gossip; *feckless*, worthless; *daut*, fondle; *tint*, lost; *asklent*, on the side; *plack*, coin; *waur bestead*, worse placed; *bienly*, warmly; *mailins*, small-holdings

Intimacy

I can be alone,
I know how to be alone.

There is a tacit understanding
between my pencils
and the trees outside;
between the rain
and my luminous hair.

The tea is boiling:
my golden zone,
my pure burning amber.

I can be alone,
I know how to be alone.
By tea-light
I write.

Translated from the Romanian by
Eva Feiler and Nina Cassian

Jewel of all islands and all almost-islands
That Neptune, fresh or salt, in clear lagoons
Or on the huge sea treasures, oh, what pleasure,
What delight at the sight of you, Sirmio, I feel,
Hardly believing it – that I'm here, safe, quit
Of boring, flat Bithynia and Thynia!
What joy compares with when the chain of cares
Snaps and the mind lays down its load, and road-
Weary, work-sore, we reach our own front door
And rest a head in the bed we have long dreamed of?
This in itself is full reward for hard
Labour. Hullo, then, beautiful Sirmio!
Be happy – your master is happy – and you, lapping
Ripples of my Etruscan lake, shake
With all the laughter lurking in your water.

Translated from the Latin by James Michie

Roundel

Now welcome Summer with thy sunnè soft,
That hast this winter's weathers overshake,
And driven away the longè nightès black.

Saint Valentine, that art full high aloft,
Thus singen smallè fowlès for thy sake;
Now welcome Summer with thy sunnè soft,
That hast this winter's weathers overshake.

Well have they causè for to gladden oft,
Since each of them recovered hath his make.
Full blissful may they singè when they wake:
Now welcome Summer with thy sunnè soft,
That hast this winter's weathers overshake,
And driven away the longè nightès black!

Reading the Book of Hills and Seas

In the month of June the grass grows high
And round my cottage thick-leaved branches sway.
There is not a bird but delights in the place where it rests;
And I too – love my thatched cottage.
I have done my ploughing;
I have sown my seed.
Again I have time to sit and read my books.
In the narrow lane there are no deep ruts;
Often my friends' carriages turn back.
In high spirits I pour out my spring wine
And pluck the lettuce growing in my garden.
A gentle rain comes stealing up from the east
And a sweet wind bears it company.
My thoughts float idly over the story of the king of Chou,
My eyes wander over the pictures of Hills and Seas.
At a single glance I survey the whole Universe.
He will never be happy, whom such pleasures fail to please!

Translated from the Chinese by Arthur Waley

On His Baldness

At dawn I sighed to see my hairs fall;
At dusk I sighed to see my hairs fall.
For I dreaded the time when the last lock should go . . .
They are all gone and I do not mind at all!
I have done with that cumbrous washing and getting dry;
My tiresome comb for ever is laid aside.
Best of all, when the weather is hot and wet,
To have no top-knot weighing down on one's head!
I put aside my messy cloth wrap;
I have got rid of my dusty tasselled fringe.
In a silver jar I have stored a cold stream,
On my bald pate I trickle a ladle full.
Like one baptized with the Water of Buddha's Law,
I sit and receive this cool, cleansing joy.
Now I know why the priest who seeks Repose
Frees his heart by first shaving his head.

Translated from the Chinese by Arthur Waley

The Hollow Tree

How oft a summer shower hath started me
To seek for shelter in a hollow tree
Old hugh ash dotterel wasted to a shell
Whose vigorous head still grew and flourished well
Where ten might sit upon the battered floor
And still look round discovering room for more
And he who chose a hermit life to share
Might have a door and make a cabin there
They seemed so like a house that our desires
Would call them so and make our gipsey fires
And eat field dinners of the juicey peas
Till we were wet and drabbled to the knees
But in our old tree house rain as it might
Not one drop fell although it rained till night

JOHN CLARE

Sabbath Bells

Ive often on a sabbath day
Where pastoral quiet dwells
Lay down among the new mown hay
To listen distant bells
That beautifully flung the sound
Upon the quiet wind
While beans in blossom breathed around
A fragrance oer the mind

A fragrance and a joy beside
That never wears away
The very air seems deified
Upon a sabbath day
So beautiful the flitting wrack
Slow pausing from the eye
Earths music seemed to call them back
Calm settled in the sky

And I have listened till I felt
A feeling not in words
A love that rudest moods would melt
When those sweet sounds was heard
A melancholly joy at rest
A pleasurable pain
A love a rapture of the breast
That nothing will explain

A dream of beauty that displays
Imaginary joys
That all the world in all its ways
Finds not to realize

All idly stretched upon the hay
The wind flirt fanning bye
How soft how sweetly swept away
The music of the sky

The ear it lost and caught the sound
Swelled beautifully on
A fitful melody around
Of sweetness heard and gone
I felt such thoughts I yearned to sing
The humming airs delight
That seemed to move the swallows wing
Into a wilder flight

The butterflye in wings of brown
Would find me where I lay
Fluttering and bobbing up and down
And settling on the hay
The waving blossoms seemed to throw
Their fragrance to the sound
While up and down and loud and low
The bells were ringing round

Evening Quatrains

The Day's grown old, the fainting Sun
Has but a little way to run,
And yet his Steeds, with all his skill,
Scarce lug the Chariot down the Hill.

With Labour spent, and Thirst opprest,
Whilst they strain hard to gain the West,
From Fetlocks hot drops melted light,
Which turn to Meteors in the Night.

The Shadows now so long do grow,
That Brambles like tall Cedars show,
Mole-hills seem Mountains, and the Ant
Appears a monstrous Elephant.

A very little little Flock
Shades thrice the ground that it would stock;
Whilst the small Stripling following them,
Appears a mighty *Polypheme*.

These being brought into the Fold,
And by the thrifty Master told,
He thinks his Wages are well paid,
Since none are either lost, or stray'd.

Now lowing Herds are each-where heard,
Chains rattle in the Villeins Yard,
The Cart's on Tayl set down to rest,
Bearing on high the Cuckolds Crest.

The hedg is stript, the Clothes brought in,
Nought's left without should be within,

The Bees are hiv'd, and hum their Charm,
Whilst every House does seem a Swarm.

The Cock now to the Roost is prest:
For he must call up all the rest;
The Sow's fast pegg'd within the Sty,
To still her squeaking Progeny.

Each one has had his Supping Mess,
The Cheese is put into the Press,
The Pans and Bowls clean scalded all,
Rear'd up against the Milk-house Wall.

And now on Benches all are sat
In the cool Air to sit and chat,
Till *Phoebus*, dipping in the West,
Shall lead the World the way to Rest.

i thank You God for most this amazing
day:for the leaping greenly spirits of trees
and a blue true dream of sky;and for everything
which is natural which is infinite which is yes

(i who have died am alive again today,
and this is the sun's birthday;this is the birth
day of life and of love and wings:and of the gay
great happening illimitably earth)

how should tasting touching hearing seeing
breathing any—lifted from the no
of all nothing—human merely being
doubt unimaginable You?

(now the ears of my ears awake and
now the eyes of my eyes are opened)

Uxor Vivamus . . .

The first night that I slept with you
And slept, I dreamt (these lines are true):
Now newly-married we had moved
Into an unkempt house we loved –
The rooms were large, the floors of stone,
The garden gently overgrown
With sunflowers, phlox, and mignonette –
All as we would have wished and yet
There was a shabby something there
Tainting the mild and windless air.
Where did it lurk? Alarmed we saw
The walls about us held the flaw –
They were of plaster, like grey chalk,
Porous and dead: it seemed our talk,
Our glances, even love, would die
With such indifference standing by.
Then, scarcely thinking what I did,
I chipped the plaster and it slid
In easy pieces to the floor;
It crumbled cleanly, more and more
Fell unresistingly away –
And there, beneath that deadening grey,
A fresco stood revealed: sky-blue
Predominated, for the view
Was an ebullient country scene,
The crowning of some pageant queen
Whose dress shone blue, and over all
The summer sky filled half the wall.
And so it was in every room,

[30]

The plaster's undistinguished gloom
Gave way to dances, festivals,
Processions, muted pastorals –
And everywhere that spacious blue:
I woke, and lying next to you
Knew all that I had dreamt was true.

May

O! the month of May, the merry month of May,
  So frolic, so gay, and so green, so green, so green!
O! and then did I unto my true Love say,
  Sweet Peg, thou shalt be my Summer's Queen.

Now the nightingale, the pretty nightingale,
  The sweetest singer in all the forest's choir,
Entreats thee, sweet Peggy, to hear thy true Love's tale:
  Lo! yonder she sitteth, her breast against a briar.

But O! I spy the cuckoo, the cuckoo, the cuckoo;
  See where she sitteth; come away, my joy:
Come away, I prithee, I do not like the cuckoo
  Should sing where my Peggy and I kiss and toy.

O! the month of May, the merry month of May,
  So frolic, so gay, and so green, so green, so green!
And then did I unto my true Love say,
  Sweet Peg, thou shalt be my Summer's Queen.

A soft Sea washed around the House
A Sea of Summer Air
And rose and fell the magic Planks
That sailed without a care –
For Captain was the Butterfly
For Helmsman was the Bee
And an entire universe
For the delighted crew.

I taste a liquor never brewed –
From Tankards scooped in Pearl –
Not all the Vats upon the Rhine
Yield such an Alcohol!

Inebriate of Air – am I –
And Debauchee of Dew –
Reeling – thro endless summer days –
From inns of Molten Blue –

When 'Landlords' turn the drunken Bee
Out of the Foxglove's door –
When Butterflies renounce their 'drams' –
I shall but drink the more!

Till Seraphs swing their snowy Hats –
And Saints – to windows run –
To see the little Tippler
Leaning against the – Sun –

Held

Not in the sense that this snapshot, a girl in a garden,
Is named for its subject, or saves her from ageing,
Not as this ammonite changed like a sinner to minerals
Heavy and cold on my palm is immortal,
But as we stopped for the sound of the lakefront one morning
Before the dawn chorus of sprinklers and starlings.

Not as this hieroglyph chiselled by Hittites in lazuli,
Spiral and faint, is a word for 'unending',
Nor as the hands, crown, and heart in the emblem of
    Claddagh,
Pewter and plain on that ring mean forever,
But as we stood at the window together, in silence,
Precisely twelve minutes by candlelight waiting for thunder.

The Sun Rising

Busy old fool, unruly sun,
    Why dost thou thus,
Through windows, and through curtains call on us?
Must to thy motions lovers' seasons run?
    Saucy pedantic wretch, go chide
    Late school-boys, and sour prentices,
  Go tell court-huntsmen, that the King will ride,
  Call country ants to harvest offices;
Love, all alike, no season knows, nor clime,
Nor hours, days, months, which are the rags of time.

Thy beams, so reverend, and strong
    Why shouldst thou think?
I could eclipse and cloud them with a wink,
But that I would not lose her sight so long:
    If her eyes have not blinded thine,
    Look, and tomorrow late, tell me,
  Whether both th'Indias of spice and mine
  Be where thou left'st them, or lie here with me.
Ask for those kings whom thou saw'st yesterday,
And thou shalt hear, All here in one bed lay.

She'is all states, and all princes, I,
    Nothing else is.
Princes do but play us; compared to this,
All honour's mimic; all wealth alchemy.
    Thou sun art half as happy as we,
    In that the world's contracted thus;
  Thine age asks ease, and since thy duties be

To warm the world, that's done in warming us.
Shine here to us, and thou art everywhere;
This bed thy centre is, these walls, thy sphere.

MAURA DOOLEY

Up on the Roof

You wonder why it is they write of it, sing of it,
till suddenly you're there, nearest you can get
to flying or jumping and you're alone, at last,
the air bright. Remembering this, I go
with my too-light jacket up to the sixth floor,
out onto the roof and I freeze under the stars
till he comes with my too-heavy jacket, heavier
and heavier, as he tries to muffle my foolishness.
A blanket on a fire (he says) and it's true
I am left black, bruised a little, smouldering.

You can sit with a book up there and reel in
life with someone else's bait. You can let your eyes
skim the river, bridges, banks, a seagull's parabola.
At night, you can watch the sky, those strange galaxies
like so many cracks in the ceiling spilling secrets
from the flat above. You can breathe. You can dream.

But he turns to me, as you'd coax a child
in the back of a stuffy car: *we could play I-Spy?*
I look at the black and blue above and the only
letter I find is 'S'. I cannot name
the dust of starlight, the pinheaded planets,
but I can join the dots to make a farming tool,
the belt of a god: all any of us needs is work,
mystery, a little time alone up on the roof.

Song

After the pangs of a desperate lover,
When day and night I have sighed all in vain,
Ah what a pleasure it is to discover
In her eyes pity, who causes my pain!

When with unkindness our love at a stand is,
And both have punished ourselves with the pain,
Ah what a pleasure the touch of her hand is,
Ah what a pleasure to press it again!

When the denial comes fainter and fainter,
And her eyes give what her tongue does deny,
Ah what a trembling I feel when I venture,
Ah what a trembling does usher my joy!

When with a sigh she accords me the blessing,
And her eyes twinkle 'twixt pleasure and pain,
Ah what a joy 'tis beyond all expressing,
Ah what a joy to hear, 'shall we again?'!

A Child's Sleep

I stood at the edge of my child's sleep
hearing her breathe;
although I could not enter there,
I could not leave.

Her sleep was a small wood,
perfumed with flowers;
dark, peaceful, sacred,
acred in hours.

And she was the spirit that lives
in the heart of such woods;
without time, without history,
wordlessly good.

I spoke her name, a pebble dropped
in the still night,
and saw her stir, both open palms
cupping their soft light;

then went to the window. The greater dark
outside the room
gazed back, maternal, wise,
with its face of moon.

HELEN DUNMORE

Privacy of rain

Rain. A plump splash
on tense, bare skin.
Rain. All the May leaves
run upward, shaking.

Rain. A first touch
at the nape of the neck.
Sharp drops kick the dust, white
downpours shudder
like curtains, rinsing
tight hairdos to innocence.

I love the privacy of rain,
the way it makes things happen
on verandahs, under canopies
or in the shelter of trees
as a door slams and a girl runs out
into the black-wet leaves.
By the brick wall an iris
sucks up the rain
like intricate food, its tongue
sherbetty, furred.

Rain. All the May leaves
run upward, shaking.
On the street, bud-silt
covers the windscreens.

10.30 a.m. Mass, June 16, 1985

When the priest made his entrance on the altar on the
    stroke of 10.30
He looked like a film star at an international airport
After having flown in from the other side of the world,
As if the other side of the world was the other side of the
    street;
Only, instead of an overnight bag slung over his shoulder,
He was carrying a chalice in its triangular green veil –
The way a dapper comedian cloaks a dove in a silk
    handkerchief.
Having kissed the altar, he strode over to the microphone:
I'd like to say how glad I am to be here with you this
    morning.

Oddly, you could see quite well that he was genuinely glad –
As if, in fact, he had been actually looking forward to
    this Sunday service,
Much the way I had been looking forward to it myself;
As if, in fact, this was the big moment of his day – of his week,
Not merely another ritual to be sanctimoniously performed.
He was a small, stocky, handsome man in his forties
With a big mop of curly grey hair
And black, horn-rimmed, tinted spectacles.
I am sure that more than half the women in the church
Fell in love with him on the spot –
Not to mention the men.
Myself, I felt like a cuddle.
The reading from the prophet Ezekiel (17: 22–24)
Was a lot of old codswallop about cedar trees in Israel
(It's a long way from a tin of steak-and-kidney pie

For Sunday lunch in a Dublin bedsit
To cedar trees in Israel),
And the epistle was even worse –
St Paul on his high horse and, as nearly always,
Putting his hoof in it – prating about 'the law court of Christ'
(Director of Public Prosecutions, Mr J. Christ, Messiah)!
With the Gospel, however, things began to look up –
The parable of the mustard seed as being the kingdom
    of heaven;
Now then the Homily, at best probably inoffensively boring.

It's Father's Day – this small, solid, serious, sexy priest
    began –
And I want to tell you about my own father
Because none of you knew him.
If there was one thing he liked, it was a pint of Guinness;
If there was one thing he liked more than a pint of Guinness
It was two pints of Guinness.
But then when he was fifty-five he gave up drink.
I never knew why, but I had my suspicions.
Long after he had died my mother told me why:
He was so proud of me when I entered the seminary
That he gave up drinking as his way of thanking God.
But he himself never said a word about it to me –
He kept his secret to the end. He died from cancer
A few weeks before I was ordained a priest.
I'd like to go to Confession – he said to me:
OK – I'll go and get a priest – I said to him:
No – don't do that – I'd prefer to talk to *you*:
Dying, he confessed to me the story of his life.
How many of you here at Mass today are fathers?
I want all of you who are fathers to stand up.

Not one male in transept or aisle or nave stood up –
It was as if all the fathers in the church had been caught out
In the profanity of their sanctity,
In the bodily nakedness of their fatherhood,
In the carnal deed of their fathering;
Then, in ones and twos and threes, fifty or sixty of us
    clambered to our feet
And blushed to the roots of our being.
Now – declared the priest – let the rest of us
Praise these men our fathers.
He began to clap hands.
Gradually the congregation began to clap hands,
Until the entire church was ablaze with clapping hands –
Wives vying with daughters, sons with sons,
Clapping clapping clapping clapping clapping,
While I stood there in a trance, tears streaming down my
    cheeks:
Jesus!
I want to tell you about my own father
Because none of you knew him!

My Mind to Me a Kingdom Is

My mind to me a kingdom is
   Such perfect joy therein I find,
That it excels all other bliss
That world affords or grows by kind.
   Though much I want which most would have,
   Yet still my mind forbids to crave.

No princely pomp, no wealthy store,
No force to win the victory,
No wily wit to salve a sore,
No shape to feed a loving eye;
   To none of these I yield as thrall,
   For why? my mind doth serve for all.

I see how plenty suffers oft,
And hasty climbers soon do fall;
I see that those which are aloft
Mishap doth threaten most of all;
   They get with toil, they keep with fear;
   Such cares my mind could never bear.

Content I live, this is my stay,
I seek no more than may suffice,
I press to bear no haughty sway;
Look, what I lack my mind supplies.
   Lo, thus I triumph like a king,
   Content with that my mind doth bring.

Some have too much, yet still do crave,
I little have, and seek no more:
They are but poor, though much they have,

And I am rich with little store:
    They poor, I rich; they beg, I give;
    They lack, I leave; they pine, I live.

I laugh not at another's loss,
I grudge not at another's gain;
No worldly waves my mind can toss,
My state at one doth still remain.
    I fear no foe, I fawn no friend;
    I loathe not life, nor dread no end.

Some weigh their pleasure by their lust,
Their wisdom by their rage of will;
Their treasure is their only trust,
A cloaked craft their store of skill:
    But all the pleasure that I find
    Is to maintain a quiet mind.

My wealth is health and perfect ease,
My conscience clear my chief defence;
I neither seek by bribes to please,
Nor by desert to breed offence.
    Thus do I live, thus will I die;
    Would all did so, as well as I.

My Ox Duke

'Twas on a summer noon, in Stainsford mead
New mown and tedded, while the weary swains,
Louting beneath an oak, their toils relieved;
And some with wanton tale the nymphs beguiled,
And some with song, and some with kisses rude;
Their scythes hung o'er their heads: when my brown ox,
Old labourer Duke, in awkward haste I saw
Run stumbling through the field to reach the shade
Of an old open barn, whose gloomy floor
The lash of sounding flails had long forgot.
In vain his eager haste: sudden old Duke
Stopped; a soft ridge of snow-white little pigs
Along the sacred threshold sleeping lay.
Burnt in the beam, and stung with swarming flies,
He stood tormented on the shadow's edge:
What should he do? What sweet forbearance held
His heavy foot from trampling on the weak,
To gain his wishes? Hither, hither all,
Ye vain, ye proud! see, humble heaven attends;
The fly-teased brute with gentle pity stays,
And shields the sleeping young. O gracious Lord!
Aid of the feeble, cheerer of distress,
In his low labyrinth each small reptile's guide!
God of unnumbered worlds! Almighty power!
Assuage our pride. Be meek, thou child of man:
Who gives thee life, gives every worm to live,
Thy kindred of the dust. – Long waiting stood
The good old labourer, in the burning beam,
And breathed upon them, nosed them, touched them soft,

With lovely fear to hurt their tender sides;
Again soft touched them; gently moved his head
From one to one; again, with touches soft,
He breathed them o'er, till gruntling waked and stared
The merry little young, their tails upcurled,
And gambolled off with scattered flight. Then sprung
The honest ox, rejoiced, into the shade.

louting, lolling

D. J. ENRIGHT

And Two Good Things

Listening to Miss Anthony, our lovely Miss,
Charming us dumb with *The Wind in the Willows*.

Dancing Sellinger's Round, and dancing and
Dancing it, and getting it perfect forever.

June 1966

Lying flat in the bracken of Richmond Park
while the legs and voices of my children pass
seeking, seeking; I remember how on the
13th of June of that simmering 1940
I was conscripted into the East Surreys,
and, more than a quarter of a century
ago, when France had fallen,
we practised concealment in this very bracken.
The burnt stalks pricked through my denims.
Hitler is now one of the antiques of History,
I lurk like a monster in my hiding place.
He didn't get me. If there were a God
it would be only polite to thank him.

7301

Learning to read you, twenty years ago,
Over the pub lunch cheese-and-onion rolls.

Learning you eat raw onions; learning your taste
For obscurity, how you encode teachers and classrooms

As *the hands, the shop-floor*; learning to hide
The sudden shining naked looks of love. And thinking

The rest of our lives, the rest of our lives
Doing perfectly ordinary things together – riding

In buses, walking in Sainsbury's, sitting
In pubs eating cheese-and-onion rolls,

All those tomorrows. Now twenty years after,
We've had seventy-three hundred of them, and

(If your arithmetic's right, and our luck) we may
Fairly reckon on seventy-three hundred more.

I hold them crammed in my arms, colossal crops
Of shining tomorrows that may never happen,

But may they! Still learning to read you,
To hear what it is you're saying, to master the code.

Morning has broken
Like the first morning,
Blackbird has spoken
Like the first bird.
Praise for the singing!
Praise for the morning!
Praise for them, springing
Fresh from the Word!

Sweet the rain's new fall
Sunlit from heaven,
Like the first dewfall
On the first grass.
Praise for the sweetness
Of the wet garden,
Sprung in completeness
Where his feet pass.

Mine is the sunlight!
Mine is the morning
Born of the one light
Eden saw play!
Praise with elation,
Praise every morning,
God's re-creation
Of the new day!

Getting Older

The first surprise: I like it.
Whatever happens now, some things
that used to terrify have not:

I didn't die young, for instance. Or lose
my only love. My three children
never had to run away from anyone.

Don't tell me this gratitude is complacent.
We all approach the edge of the same blackness
which for me is silent.

Knowing as much sharpens
my delight in January freesia,
hot coffee, winter sunlight. So we say

as we lie close on some gentle occasion:
every day won from such
darkness is a celebration.

Mowing

There was never a sound beside the wood but one,
And that was my long scythe whispering to the ground.
What was it it whispered? I knew not well myself;
Perhaps it was something about the heat of the sun,
Something, perhaps, about the lack of sound –
And that was why it whispered and did not speak.
It was no dream of the gift of idle hours,
Or easy gold at the hand of fay or elf:
Anything more than the truth would have seemed too weak
To the earnest love that laid the swale in rows,
Not without feeble-pointed spikes of flowers
(Pale orchises), and scared a bright green snake.
The fact is the sweetest dream that labor knows.
My long scythe whispered and left the hay to make.

Matins

Not the sun merely but the earth
itself shines, white fire
leaping from the showy mountains
and the flat road
shimmering in early morning: is this
for us only, to induce
response, or are you
stirred also, helpless
to control yourself
in earth's presence – I am ashamed
at what I thought you were,
distant from us, regarding us
as an experiment: it is
a bitter thing to be
the disposable animal,
a bitter thing. Dear friend,
dear trembling partner, what
surprises you most in what you feel,
earth's radiance or your own delight?
For me, always
the delight is the surprise.

Song: The Palm Tree

Palm-tree, single and apart
　In your serpent-haunted land,
Like the fountain of a heart
　Soaring into air from sand –
None can count it as a fault
That your roots are fed with salt.

Panniers-full of dates you yield,
　Thorny branches laced with light,
Wistful for no pasture-field
　Fed by torrents from a height,
Short of politics to share
With the damson or the pear.

Never-failing phoenix tree
　In your serpent-haunted land,
Fount of magic soaring free
　From a desert of salt sand;
Tears of joy are salty too –
Mine shall flow in praise of you.

Sweet Things

He licks the last chocolate ice cream
from the scabbed corners of his mouth.
Sitting in the sun on a step
outside the laundromat,
mongoloid Don turns his crewcut head
and spies me coming down the street.
'Hi!' He says it with the mannered
enthusiasm of a fraternity brother.
'Take me cross the street!?' part
question part command. I hold
the sticky bunch of small fingers in mine
and we stumble across. They sell
peaches and pears over there,
the juice will dribble down your chin.
He turns before I leave him,
saying abruptly with the same
mixture of order and request
'Gimme a quarter!?' I
don't give it, never have, not to him,
I wonder why not, and as I
walk on alone I realize
it's because his unripened mind
never recognizes me, me
for myself, he only says hi
for what he can get, quarters to
buy sweet things, one after another,
he goes from store to store, from
candy store to ice cream store to
bakery to produce market, unending

[57]

quest for the palate's pleasure. Then
out to panhandle again,
more quarters, more sweet things.
My errands are toothpaste,
vitamin pills and a book of stamps.
No self-indulgence there.
But who's this coming up? It's
John, no Chuck, how
could his name have slipped my mind.
Chuck gives a one-sided smile, he stands
as if fresh from a laundromat,
a scrubbed cowboy, Tom Sawyer
grown up, yet stylish, perhaps
even careful, his dark hair
slicked back in the latest manner.
When he shakes my hand I feel
a dry finger playfully bending inward
and touching my palm in secret.
'It's a long time
since we got together,' says John.
Chuck, that is. The warm teasing
tickle in the cave of our handshake
took my mind off toothpaste,
snatched it off, indeed.
How handsome he is in
his lust and energy, in his
fine display of impulse.
Boldly 'How about now?' I say
knowing the answer. My boy
I could eat you whole. In the long pause
I gaze at him up and down and
from his blue sneakers back to the redawning
one-sided smile. We know our charm.

We know delay makes pleasure great.
In our eyes, on our tongues,
we savour the approaching delight
of things we know yet are fresh always.
Sweet things. Sweet things.

Ice on the Highway

Seven buxom women abreast, and arm in arm,
  Trudge down the hill, tip-toed,
   And breathing warm;
They must perforce trudge thus, to keep upright
  On the glassy ice-bound road,

And they must get to market whether or no,
  Provisions running low
  With the nearing Saturday night,
While the lumbering van wherein they mostly ride
   Can nowise go:
Yet loud their laughter as they stagger and slide!

The Skylight

You were the one for skylights. I opposed
Cutting into the seasoned tongue-and-groove
Of pitch pine. I liked it low and closed,
Its claustrophobic, nest-up-in-the-roof
Effect. I liked the snuff-dry feeling,
The perfect, trunk-lid fit of the old ceiling.
Under there, it was all hutch and hatch.
The blue slates kept the heat like midnight thatch.

But when the slates came off, extravagant
Sky entered and held surprise wide open.
For days I felt like an inhabitant
Of that house where the man sick of the palsy
Was lowered through the roof, had his sins forgiven,
Was healed, took up his bed and walked away.

The Rain Stick

for Beth and Rand

Upend the rain stick and what happens next
Is a music that you never would have known
To listen for. In a cactus stalk

Downpour, sluice-rush, spillage and backwash
Come flowing through. You stand there like a pipe
Being played by water, you shake it again lightly

And diminuendo runs through all its scales
Like a gutter stopping trickling. And now here comes
A sprinkle of drops out of the freshened leaves,

Then subtle little wets off grass and daisies;
Then glitter-drizzle, almost-breaths of air.
Upend the stick again. What happens next

Is undiminished for having happened once,
Twice, ten, a thousand times before.
Who cares if all the music that transpires

Is the fall of grit or dry seeds through a cactus?
You are like a rich man entering heaven
Through the ear of a raindrop. Listen now again.

Thanksgiving

Now the god looks down with favour,
Shall I not say I'm delighted,
Having made such lamentations
When my love was unrequited

That a thousand lads wrote verses
In the same despairing fashion,
Causing far more trouble than was
Caused to start with by my passion?

Oh you nightingales within me,
Chorus now this revelation,
Tell your joy to every hearer
In full-hearted celebration.

Translated from the German by T. J. Reid and David Cram

Church-Music

Sweetest of sweets, I thank you: when displeasure
    Did through my body wound my mind,
You took me thence, and in your house of pleasure
    A dainty lodging me assigned.

Now I in you without a body move,
    Rising and falling with your wings:
We both together sweetly live and love,
    Yet say sometimes, *God help poor Kings.*

Comfort, I'll die; for if you post from me,
    Sure I shall do so, and much more:
But if I travel in your company,
    You know the way to heaven's door.

Prayer

Prayer the Churches banquet, Angels age,
   Gods breath in man returning to his birth,
   The soul in paraphrase, heart in pilgrimage,
The Christian plummet sounding heav'n and earth;

Engine against th' Almightie, sinners towre,
   Reversed thunder, Christ-side-piercing spear,
   The six-daies – world transposing in an houre,
A kinde of tune, which all things heare and fear;

Softnesse, and peace, and joy, and love, and blisse,
   Exalted Manna, gladnesse of the best,
   Heaven in ordinarie, man well drest,
The milkie may, the bird of Paradise,
   Church-bels beyond the starres heard, the souls bloud,
   The land of spices; something understood.

His Grange, or private wealth

    Though Clock,
To tell how night drawes hence, I've none,
      A Cock,
I have, to sing how day drawes on.
      I have
A maid (my *Prew*) by good luck sent,
      To save
That little, Fates me gave or lent.
      A Hen
I keep, which creeking day by day,
      Tells when
She goes her long white egg to lay.
      A goose
I have, which, with a jealous eare,
      Lets loose
Her tongue, to tell what danger's neare.
      A Lamb
I keep (tame) with my morsells fed,
      Whose Dam
An Orphan left him (lately dead.)
      A Cat
I keep, that playes about my House,
      Grown fat,
With eating many a miching Mouse.
      To these
A *Trasy** I do keep, whereby
      I please
The more my rurall privacie:
      Which are

But toyes, to give my heart some ease:
            Where care
None is, slight things do lightly please.

*His Spaniel

The Seasons

Ere the beard of thistle sails,
Ere the tadpoles wag their tails;
When the maids with milking-pails
Doff their mits and blow their nails;
When the cottage chimney smokes,
And wanton greybeards crack their jokes
By the glowing ember's light,
And scare the girls with tale of sprite;
Then will we, o'er ale and cakes,
Brag of feats at autumn wakes.

When the swallows twittering sing
Of the lovely birth of spring;
When bridegrooms make our three bells ring,
Ding dong ding – ding dong ding;
When the valley's face is seen
Veiled in many a shade of green;
When girls of husbands nightly dream,
And jolly swains get clouted cream;
Then we, upon sweet primrose beds,
Will troll our glees and rest our heads.

When the young frog fears the rook,
When the kine stand in the brook;
When sleepy louts lose many a crook,
And codlings drop when trees are shook;
When salt mushrooms nightly spring,
And martins dip the dappled wing;
When the sun with straight-down beam
Lathers well the lusty team;

Then beneath new hay-ricks we
Will sing with might and merry glee.

When the sickle and the scythe
Make the ruddy farmer blithe;
When Hodge the bulky sheaf doth writhe,
And our fat Vicar claims his tithe;
When autumn yields her golden store,
Till well-filled barns can hold no more;
When ripe fruits press the plenteous board,
And old wives cull their wintry hoard;
Then will we, when labour's o'er,
At harvest-home our catches roar.

writhe, bind

Pied Beauty

Glory be to God for dappled things –
   For skies of couple-colour as a brinded cow;
   For rose-moles all in stipple upon trout that swim;
Fresh-firecoal chestnut-falls; finches' wings;
   Landscape plotted and pieced – fold, fallow, and plough;
   And áll trádes, their gear and tackle and trim.

All things counter, original, spare, strange;
   Whatever is fickle, freckled (who knows how?)
   With swift, slow; sweet, sour; adazzle, dim;
He fathers-forth whose beauty is past change:
                  Praise him.

Harlem Night Song

Come,
Let us roam the night together
Singing.

I love you.

Across
The Harlem roof-tops
Moon is shining.
Night sky is blue.
Stars are great drops
Of golden dew.

Down the street
A band is playing.

I love you.

Come,
Let us roam the night together
Singing.

Full Moon and Little Frieda

A cool small evening shrunk to a dog bark and the clank of
    a bucket –

And you listening.
A spider's web, tense for the dew's touch.
A pail lifted, still and brimming – mirror
To tempt a first star to a tremor.

Cows are going home in the lane there, looping the hedges
    with their warm wreaths of breath –
A dark river of blood, many boulders,
Balancing unspilled milk.

'Moon!' you cry suddenly, 'Moon! Moon!'

The moon has stepped back like an artist gazing amazed at
    a work

That points at him amazed.

Jenny Kiss'd Me

Jenny kiss'd me when we met,
Jumping from the chair she sat in;
Time, you thief, who love to get
Sweets into your list, put that in!
Say I'm weary, say I'm sad,
Say that health and wealth have miss'd me,
Say I'm growing old, but add
Jenny kiss'd me.

The Way We Live

Pass the tambourine, let me bash out praises
to the Lord God of movement, to Absolute
non-friction, flight, and the scarey side:
death by avalanche, birth by failed contraception.
Of chicken tandoori and reggae, loud, from tenements,
commitment, driving fast and unswerving
friendship. Of tee-shirts on pulleys, giros and Bombay,
barmen, dreaming waitresses with many fake-gold
bangles. Or airports, impulse, and waking to uncertainty,
to strip-lights, motorways, or that pantheon –
the mountains. To overdrafts and grafting

and the fit slow pulse of wipers as you're
creeping over Rannoch, while the God of moorland
walks abroad with his entourage of freezing fog,
his bodyguard of snow.
Of endless gloaming in the North, of Asiatic swelter,
to launderettes, anecdotes, passions and exhaustion,
Final Demands and dead men, the skeletal grip
of government. To misery and elation; mixed,
the sod and caprice of landlords.
To the way it fits, the way it is, the way it seems
to be: let me bash out praises – pass the tambourine.

Hymn

Room, room, make room for the bouncing belly,
First father of sauce, and deviser of jelly,
Prime master of arts, and the giver of wit,
That found out the excellent engine, the spit,
The plough, and the flail, the mill, and the hopper,
The hutch, and the boulter, the furnace, and copper,
The oven, the bavin, the mawkin, the peel,
The hearth, and the range, the dog and the wheel,
He, he first invented the hogshead and tun,
The gimlet and vice too, and taught 'em to run.
And since, with the funnel, an Hippocras bag
He's made of himself, that now he cries swag.
Which shows, though the pleasure be but of four inches,
Yet he is a weasel, the gullet that pinches,
Of any delight, and not spares from the back
Whatever to make of the belly a sack.
Hail, hail, plump paunch, O the founder of taste
For fresh meats, or powdered, or pickle, or paste;
Devourer of broiled, baked, roasted or sod,
And emptier of cups, be they even or odd;
All which have now made thee so wide in the waist
As scarce with no pudding thou art to be laced;
But eating and drinking until thou dost nod,
Thou break'st all thy girdles, and break'st forth a god.

On First Looking into Chapman's Homer

Much have I travell'd in the realms of gold,
    And many goodly states and kingdoms seen;
    Round many western islands have I been
Which bards in fealty to Apollo hold.
Oft of one wide expanse had I been told
    That deep-brow'd Homer ruled as his demesne;
    Yet did I never breathe its pure serene
Till I heard Chapman speak out loud and bold:
Then felt I like some watcher of the skies
    When a new planet swims into his ken;
Or like stout Cortez when with eagle eyes
    He star'd at the Pacific – and all his men
Look'd at each other with a wild surmise –
    Silent, upon a peak in Darien.

For Sidney Bechet

That note you hold, narrowing and rising, shakes
Like New Orleans reflected on the water,
And in all ears appropriate falsehood wakes,

Building for some a legendary Quarter
Of balconies, flower-baskets and quadrilles,
Everyone making love and going shares –

Oh, play that thing! Mute glorious Storyvilles
Others may license, grouping round their chairs
Sporting-house girls like circus tigers (priced

Far above rubies) to pretend their fads,
While scholars *manqués* nod around unnoticed
Wrapped up in personnels like old plaids.

On me your voice falls as they say love should,
Like an enormous yes. My Crescent City
Is where your speech alone is understood,

And greeted as the natural noise of good,
Scattering long-haired grief and scored pity.

To Althea, from Prison

When Love with unconfinèd wings
   Hovers within my gates;
And my divine Althea brings
   To whisper at the grates;
When I lie tangled in her hair,
   And fettered to her eye;
The Gods that wanton in the air
   Know no such liberty.

When flowing cups run swiftly round
   With no allaying Thames,
Our careless heads with roses bound
   Our hearts with loyal flames;
When thirsty grief in wine we steep,
   When healths and draughts go free,
Fishes that tipple in the deep
   Know no such liberty.

When, like committed linnets, I
   With shriller throat shall sing
The sweetness, mercy, majesty,
   And glories of my King;
When I shall voice aloud how good
   He is, how great should be,
Enlargèd winds that curl the flood
   Know no such liberty.

Stone walls do not a prison make,
   Nor iron bars a cage;
Minds innocent and quiet take
   That for an hermitage;

If I have freedom in my love,
  And in my soul am free;
Angels alone that soar above
  Enjoy such liberty.

Small Rain

The rain – it was a little rain – walked through the wood
    (a little wood)
Leaving behind unexpected decorations and delicacies
On the fox by the dyke, that was eating a salmon's head.
(The poacher who had hidden it wasn't going to be
    pleased.)

The rain whisperingly went on, past the cliff all Picasso'd
With profiles, blackening the Stoer peat stacks, silvering
Forty sheep's backs, half smudging out a buzzard.
It reached us. It passed us, totally unimpressed.

Not me. I looked at you, all cobwebby with seeds of water,
Changed from Summer to Spring. I had absolutely no way
    of saying
How vivid can be unemphatic, how bright can be brighter
Than brightness. You knew, though. You were smiling,
    and no wonder.

NORMAN MACCAIG

Ballade of Good Whisky

You whose ambition is to swim the Minch
Or write a drum concerto in B flat
Or run like Bannister or box like Lynch
Or find the Ark wrecked on Mt Ararat –
No special training's needed: thin or fat,
You'll do it if you never once supplant
As basis of your commissariat
Glenfiddich, Bruichladdich and Glengrant.

My own desires are small. In fact, I flinch
From heaving a heavenly Hindu from her ghat
Or hauling Loch Ness monsters, inch by inch,
Out of their wild and watery habitat.
I've no desire to be Jehoshaphat
Or toy with houris fetched from the Levant.
But give to me – *bis dat qui cito dat* –
Glenfiddich, Bruichladdich and Glengrant.

I would drink down, and think the feat a cinch,
The Congo, Volga, Amazon, La Platte,
And Tweed as chaser – a bargain, this, to clinch
In spite of *nota bene* and *caveat*
(Though what a feast must follow after that
Of Amplex, the divine deodorant!) –
If they ran – hear my heart go pit-a-pat! –
Glenfiddich, Bruichladdich and Glengrant.

Envoi
Chris! (whether perpendicular or flat
Or moving rather horribly aslant)
Here is a toast that you won't scunner at –
Glenfiddich, Bruichladdich and Glengrant!

Elegia V

Corinnae concubitus

In summer's heat, and mid-time of the day,
To rest my limbs upon a bed I lay;
One window shut, the other open stood,
Which gave such light as twinkles in a wood,
Like twilight glimpse at setting of the sun,
Or night being past, and yet not day begun.
Such light to shamefast maidens must be shown,
Where they may sport and seem to be unknown.
Then came Corinna in a long loose gown,
Her white neck hid with tresses hanging down,
Resembling fair Semiramis going to bed,
Or Lais of a thousand wooers sped.
I snatched her gown; being thin, the harm was small,
Yet strived she to be covered therewithal,
And striving thus as one that would be cast,
Betrayed herself, and yielded at the last.
Stark naked as she stood before mine eye,
Not one wen in her body could I spy.
What arms and shoulders did I touch and see,
How apt her breasts were to be pressed by me!
How smooth a belly under her waist saw I,
How large a leg, and what a lusty thigh!
To leave the rest, all liked me passing well;
I clinged her naked body, down she fell.
Judge you the rest: being tired she bade me kiss;
Jove send me more such afternoons as this.

ANDREW MARVELL

The Garden

How vainly men themselves amaze
To win the palm, the oak, or bays;
And their incessant labours see
Crowned from some single herb, or tree,
Whose short and narrow-vergèd shade
Does prudently their toils upbraid;
While all flow'rs and all trees do close
To weave the garlands of repose.

Fair Quiet, have I found thee here,
And Innocence, thy sister dear?
Mistaken long, I sought you then
In busy companies of men.
Your sacred plants, if here below,
Only among the plants will grow;
Society is all but rude
To this delicious solitude.

No white nor red was ever seen
So amorous as this lovely green.
Fond lovers, cruel as their flame,
Cut in these trees their mistress' name:
Little, alas! they know or heed
How far these beauties hers exceed!
Fair trees! wheres'e'er your barks I wound
No name shall but your own be found.

When we have run our passion's heat,
Love hither makes his best retreat.
The Gods, that mortal beauty chase,
Still in a tree did end their race;

Apollo hunted Daphne so,
Only that she might laurel grow;
And Pan did after Syrinx speed,
Not as a nymph, but for a reed.

What wondrous life is this I lead!
Ripe apples drop about my head;
The luscious clusters of the vine
Upon my mouth do crush their wine;
The nectaren, and curious peach,
Into my hands themselves do reach;
Stumbling on melons, as I pass,
Insnared with flowers, I fall on grass.

Meanwhile, the mind, from pleasure less,
Withdraws into its happiness:
The mind, that ocean where each kind
Does straight its own resemblance find;
Yet it creates, transcending these,
Far other worlds, and other seas;
Annihilating all that's made
To a green thought in a green shade.

Here at the fountain's sliding foot,
Or at some fruit-tree's mossy root,
Casting the body's vest aside,
My soul into the boughs does glide:
There like a bird it sits, and sings,
Then whets and claps its silver wings;
And, till prepared for longer flight,
Waves in its plumes the various light.

Such was that happy garden-state,
While man there walked without a mate:
After a place so pure and sweet,

What other help could yet be meet!
But 'twas beyond a mortal's share
To wander solitary there:
Two paradises 'twere in one,
To live in paradise alone!

How well the skilful gardener drew
Of flowers, and herbs, this dial new;
Where, from above, the milder sun
Does through a fragrant zodiac run;
And, as it works, the industrious bee
Computes its time as well as we.
How could such sweet and wholesome hours
Be reckon'd but with herbs and flowers!

Recuerdo

We were very tired, we were very merry –
We had gone back and forth all night on the ferry.
It was bare and bright, and smelled like a stable –
But we looked into a fire, we leaned across a table,
We lay on a hill-top underneath the moon;
And the whistles kept blowing, and the dawn came soon.

We were very tired, we were very merry –
We had gone back and forth all night on the ferry;
And you ate an apple, and I ate a pear,
From a dozen of each we had bought somewhere;
And the sky went wan, and the wind came cold,
And the sun rose dripping, a bucketful of gold.

We were very tired, we were very merry,
We had gone back and forth all night on the ferry.
We hailed, 'Good morrow, mother!' to a shawl-covered head,
And bought a morning paper, which neither of us read;
And she wept, 'God bless you!' for the apples and pears,
And we gave her all our money but our subway fares.

Blacksmith Shop

I liked the bellows operated by rope.
A hand or foot pedal – I don't remember which.
But that blowing, and the blazing of the fire!
And a piece of iron in the fire, held there by tongs,
Red, softened for the anvil,
Beaten with a hammer, bent into a horseshoe,
Thrown in a bucket of water, sizzle, steam.

And horses hitched to be shod,
Tossing their manes; and in the grass by the river
Plowshares, sledge runners, harrows waiting for repair

At the entrance, my bare feet on the dirt floor,
Here, gusts of heat; at my back, white clouds.
I stare and stare. It seems I was called for this:
To glorify things just because they are.

Translated from the Polish by the author and Robert Hass

One Cigarette

No smoke without you, my fire.
After you left,
your cigarette glowed on in my ashtray
and sent up a long thread of such quiet grey
I smiled to wonder who would believe its signal
of so much love. One cigarette
in the non-smoker's tray.
As the last spire
trembles up, a sudden draught
blows it winding into my face.
Is it smell, is it taste?
You are here again, and I am drunk on your tobacco lips.
Out with the light.
Let the smoke lie back in the dark.
Till I hear the very ash
sigh down among the flowers of brass
I'll breathe, and long past midnight, your last kiss.

You Do, I Do

The Easter night they threw the bedsprings on the fire in
Argentina, what the bedsprings meant to you was food –
a giant grill. *Meat ladled from a barrow by two men*
with shovels, sweetheart, like the ones for pizzas:
veal and pork and lamb and beef and beef and beef.

Unknown to me, you hugged your knees, cross-legged,
and hoped the obvious and mad would come to pass.
It did: your charlady, for instance, and a taxi-driver,
lurching up to tango in a tango quite unlike the one we
know – 'Come Dancing', and all that. More like fucking

and a knife-fight rolled in one. You understand?
I do. I see you smile, half-skeletal and half-encouraged
in the juicy flames, and feel the eyes of strangers burning
on your mouth and arms and neck. The man beside you,
when the dance is over, thinks you'll be returning to his flat.

Our envies draw us further into love. Not only envies,
but they're part of it. And so, before your story ends,
you're propped up on one elbow in our crumpled bed
and asking me where I'd have been that night: alone,
I tell you, dozing in a frozen room – too tired for sleep,

and interrupted sometimes by that couple on the floor below
(those creaking shrieks, as though he might be winged
and lightly jumping on her from a wardrobe), sometimes
by the warning-buoy left groaning on the river streets away:
Don't come near me. Don't come near me. Don't . . . But why,

with so much water underneath the bridge,
should this concern us now? The instant I roll over,

press you gently back against the pillow,
stroke your hair out in its silky, spiky crown,
and stare into your face, I feel a stranger to myself

and all the lives I've led – like someone travelling,
whose boat has suddenly stood off a sunlit coast
with him on deck, who never saw these cliffs before,
or smelt this new-mown grass smell drifting out to sea,
but knows at once that he belongs here, and he's home.

The Confirmation

Yes, yours, my love, is the right human face.
I in my mind had waited for this long,
Seeing the false and searching for the true,
Then found you as a traveller finds a place
Of welcome suddenly amid the wrong
Valleys and rocks and twisting roads. But you,
What shall I call you? A fountain in a waste,
A well of water in a country dry,
Or anything that's honest and good, an eye
That makes the whole world bright. Your open heart,
Simple with giving, gives the primal deed,
The first good world, the blossom, the blowing seed,
The hearth, the steadfast land, the wandering sea,
Not beautiful or rare in every part,
But like yourself, as they were meant to be.

Spring Hail

This is for spring and hail, that you may remember:
for a boy long ago, and a pony that could fly.

We had huddled together a long time in the shed
in the scent of vanished corn and wild bush birds,
and then the hammering faltered, and the torn
cobwebs ceased their quivering and hung still
from the nested rafters. We became uneasy
at the silence that grew about us, and came out.

The beaded violence had ceased. Fresh-minted hills
smoked, and the heavens swirled and blew away.
The paddocks were endless again, and all around
leaves lay beneath their trees, and cakes of moss.
Sheep trotted and propped, and shook out ice from their
    wool.
The hard blue highway that had carried us there
fumed as we crossed it, and the hail I scooped
from underfoot still bore the taste of sky
and hurt my teeth, and crackled as we walked.

This is for spring and hail, that you may remember
a boy long ago, and a pony that could fly.

With the creak and stop of a gate, we started to trespass:
my pony bent his head and drank up grass
while I ate ice, and wandered, and ate ice.
There was a peach tree growing wild by a bank
and under it and round, sweet dented fruit
weeping pale juice amongst hail-shotten leaves,
and this I picked up and ate till I was filled.

I sat on a log then, listening with my skin
to the secret feast of the sun, to the long wet worms
at work in the earth, and, deeper down, the stones
beneath the earth, uneasy that their sleep
should be troubled by dreams of water soaking down,
and I heard with my ears the creek on its bed of mould
moving and passing with a mothering sound.

This is for spring and hail, that you may remember
a boy long ago on a pony that could fly.

My pony came up then and stood by me,
waiting to be gone. The sky was now
spotless from dome to earth, and balanced there
on the cutting-edge of mountains. It was time
to leap to the saddle and go, a thunderbolt whirling
sheep and saplings behind, and the rearing fence
that we took at a bound, and the old, abandoned shed
forgotten behind, and the paddock forgotten behind.
Time to shatter peace and lean into spring
as into a battering wind, and be rapidly gone.

It was time, high time, the highest and only time
to stand in the stirrups and shout out, blind with wind
for the height and clatter of ridges to be topped
and the racing downward after through the lands
of floating green and bridges and flickering trees.
It was time, as never again it was time
to pull the bridle up, so the racketing hooves
fell silent as we ascended from the hill
above the farms, far up to where the hail
formed and hung weightless in the upper air,
charting the birdless winds with silver roads
for us to follow and be utterly gone.

This is for spring and hail, that you may remember
a boy and a pony long ago who could fly.

Shower

From the metal poppy
this good blast of trance
arriving as shock, private cloudburst blazing down,
worst in a boarding-house greased tub, or a barrack with
    competitions,
best in a stall, this enveloping passion of Australians:
tropics that sweat for you, torrent that braces with its heat,
inflames you with its chill, action sauna, inverse bidet,
sleek vertical coruscating ghost of your inner river,
reminding all your fluids, streaming off your points,
    awakening
the tacky soap to blossom and ripe autumn, releasing the
    squeezed gardens,
smoky valet smoothing your impalpable overnight
    pyjamas off,
pillar you can step through, force-field absolving love's
    efforts,
nicest yard of the jogging track, speeding aeroplane
    minutely
steered with two controls, or trimmed with a knurled wheel.
Some people like to still this energy and lie in it,
stirring circles with their pleasure in it – but my delight's
    that toga
worn on either or both shoulders, fluted drapery, silk
    whispering to the tiles
with its spiralling frothy hem continuous round the
    gurgle-hole;
this ecstatic partner, dreamy to dance in slow embrace with
after factory-floor rock, or even to meet as Lot's abstracted

merciful wife on a rusty ship in dog latitudes,
sweetest dressing of the day in the dusty bush, this persistent
time-capsule of unwinding, this nimble straight
    well-wisher.
Only in England is its name an unkind word;
only in Europe is it enjoyed by telephone.

On Her Way to Recovery

My thirteen-year-old daughter
is now taller than me.
Illness seemed to have stretched her a bit.

She, who was on her back
for four days and four nights,
feverish, heavy limbed, uneating,

Got up this morning
pulled on her sneakers, my long red dressing gown,
and went out into the garden.

'Don't worry,' she says,
coming suddenly into the room
where I'm lying, 'I dressed warm.'

Startled. Pleased.
I glance up at the red-robed gazelle
on her way to recovery.

FRANK O'HARA

Autobiographia Literaria

When I was a child
I played by myself in a
corner of the schoolyard
all alone.

I hated dolls and I
hated games, animals were
not friendly and birds
flew away.

If anyone was looking
for me I hid behind a
tree and cried out 'I am
an orphan.'

And here I am, the
center of all beauty!
writing these poems!
Imagine!

Magna est Veritas

Here, in this little Bay,
Full of tumultuous life and great repose,
Where, twice a day,
The purposeless, glad ocean comes and goes,
Under high cliffs, and far from the huge town,
I sit me down.
For want of me the world's course will not fail:
When all its work is done, the lie shall rot;
The truth is great, and shall prevail,
When none cares whether it prevail or not.

GEORGE PEELE

Song

When as the rye reach to the chin,
   And chopcherry, chopcherry ripe within,
Strawberries swimming in the cream,
And school-boys playing in the stream;
   Then O, then O, then O my true love said,
    Till that time come again,
   She could not live a maid.

You're

Clownlike, happiest on your hands,
Feet to the stars, and moon-skulled,
Gilled like a fish. A common-sense
Thumbs-down on the dodo's mode.
Wrapped up in yourself like a spool,
Trawling your dark as owls do.
Mute as a turnip from the Fourth
Of July to All Fools' Day,
O high-riser, my little loaf.

Vague as fog and looked for like mail.
Farther off than Australia.
Bent-backed Atlas, our travelled prawn.
Snug as a bud and at home
Like a sprat in a pickle jug.
A creel of eels, all ripples.
Jumpy as a Mexican bean.
Right, like a well-done sum.
A clean slate, with your own face on.

Toast

When I'm old, I'll say *the summer*
they built the stadium. And I won't mean

the council. I'll be hugging the memory
of how, open to sun and the judgement

of passing eyes, young builders lay
golden and melting on hot pavements,

the toast of Cardiff. Each blessed lunchtime
Westgate Street, St John's, the Hayes

were lined with fit bodies; forget
the jokes, these jeans were fuzz stretched tight

over unripe peaches. Sex objects,
and happily up for it. When women

sauntered by, whistling, they'd bask
in warm smiles, browning slowly, loving

the light. Sometimes they'd clock men
looking them over. It made no odds;

they never got mad; it was too heady
being young and fancied and in the sun.

They're gone now; all we have left of them
this vast concrete-and-glass mother-ship

that seems to have landed awkwardly
in our midst. And Westgate's dark

with November rain, but different, as if
the stones retain heat, secret impressions

of shoulder-blades, shallow cups,
as sand would do. The grey façade

of the empty auction house, three storeys
of boarded windows, doesn't look sad,

more like it's closed its eyes, breathing in
the smell of sweat, sunblock, confidence.

Heaven on Earth

Now that it is night,
you fetch in the washing
from outer space,

from the frozen garden
filmed like a kidney,
with a ghost in your mouth,

and everything you hold,
two floating shirts, a sheet,
ignores the law of gravity.

Only this morning,
the wren at her millinery,
making a baby's soft bonnet,

as we stopped by the spring,
watching the water
well up in the grass,

as if the world were teething.
It was heaven on earth
and it was only the morning.

The South

from Katerina Brac

The insects formed an *a cappella* choir
and praised God for his almighty heat.
Their song hung like a backcloth,
a seamless silvery-tremulous weaving of sound.
We staggered about like new angels, amazed
at the dazzle and torpor of Paradise.

Lizards paddled on the walls of the house.
Some of the birds could speak a word or two
in our language. A black caterpillar
on its curtain-fringe of little red legs
crossed my path by means of a repeated self-strumming –
a charmed creature, not to be crushed underfoot.

Fed by a system of hidden streams,
there was a rock pool, emerald-green
by daylight, malachite at dusk.
We dipped into this chill element
as if it were possible to taste a little
of whatever spiritual existence we cared to try.

I hesitate to say that I was too lucky,
but what is one to make of experiences
that felt like memory even as they happened?
There were mosquitoes, but their gloating hover
never touched me, and night-lightning
fluttered harmlessly at the horizon.

A Birthday

My heart is like a singing bird
  Whose nest is in a watered shoot:
My heart is like an apple-tree
  Whose boughs are bent with thickset fruit;
My heart is like a rainbow shell
  That paddles in a halcyon sea;
My heart is gladder than all these
  Because my love is come to me.

Raise me a dais of silk and down;
  Hang it with vair and purple dyes;
Carve it in doves and pomegranates,
  And peacocks with a hundred eyes;
Work it in gold and silver grapes,
  In leaves and silver fleurs-de-lys;
Because the birthday of my life
  Is come, my love is come to me.

Bad-tempered, I got back:
Then, in the garden,
The willow-tree.

Translated from the Japanese by
Geoffrey Bownas and Anthony Thwaite

Everyone Sang

Everyone suddenly burst out singing;
And I was filled with such delight
As prisoned birds must find in freedom,
Winging wildly across the white
Orchards and dark-green fields; on – on – and out of sight.

Everyone's voice was suddenly lifted;
And beauty came like the setting sun:
My heart was shaken with tears; and horror
Drifted away . . . O, but Everyone
Was a bird; and the song was wordless; the singing will
    never be done.

Fauré's Second Piano Quartet

On a day like this the rain comes
down in fat and random drops among
the ailanthus leaves – 'the tree
of Heaven' – the leaves that on moon-
lit nights shimmer black and blade-
shaped at this third-floor window.
And there are bunches of small green
knobs, buds, crowded together. The
rapid music fills in the spaces of
the leaves. And the piano comes in,
like an extra heartbeat, dangerous
and lovely. Slower now, less like
the leaves, more like the rain which
almost isn't rain, more like thawed-
out hail. All this beauty in the
mess of this small apartment on
West 20th in Chelsea, New York.
Slowly the notes pour out, slowly,
more slowly still, fat rain falls.

Delicious Babies

Because of spring there are babies everywhere,
sweet or sulky, irascible or full of the milk of human
    kindness.
Yum, yum! Delicious babies!
Babies with the soft skins of babies, cheeks
of such tit-bit pinkness, tickle-able babies, tasty babies,
mouth-watering babies.

The pads of their hands! The rounds
of their knees! Their good smells of bathtime
and new clothes and gobbled rusks!
Even their discarded nappies are worthy of them, reveal
    their powers.
Legions and hosts of babies! Babies bold as lions, sighing
    babies,
tricksy babies, omniscient babies, babies using a plain
    language
of reasonable demands and courteous acceptance.
Others have the habit of loud contradiction,
can empty a railway carriage (though their displeasing
    howls
cheer up childless women).
Look at this baby, sitting bolt upright in his buggy!
Consider his lofty unsmiling acknowledgement of our
    adulation,

look at the elfin golfer's hat flattering his fluffy hair!
Look next at this very smallest of babies
tightly wrapped in a foppery of blankets.
In his high promenading pram he sleeps sumptuously,

only a nose, his father's, a white bonnet and a wink
of eyelid showing.

All babies are manic-serene, all babies are mine,
all babies are edible, the boys taste best.
I feed on them, nectareous are my babies,
manna, confiture, my sweet groceries.

I smack my lips,
deep in my belly the egg ripens,
makes the windows shake,
another ovum-quake
moves earth, sky and me . . .

Bring me more babies! Let me have them for breakfast,
lunch and tea! Let me feast, let my honey-banquet of babies
go on forever, fresh deliveries night and day!

On Taking a Batchelor's Degree

Exegi monumentum ære perennius, &c.
Horace, *Od., iii, 30.*

'Tis done: – I tow'r to that degree,
   And catch such heav'nly fire,
That HORACE ne'er could rant like me,
   Nor is *King's* chapel higher. –
My name in sure recording page
   Shall time itself o'erpow'r,
If no rude mice with envious rage
   The buttery books devour.
A title too with added grace,
   My name shall now attend,
Till to the church with silent pace
   A nymph and priest ascend.
Ev'n in the schools I now rejoice,
   Where late I shook with fear,
Nor heed the *Moderator's* voice
   Loud thundering in my ear.
Then with *Æolian* flute I blow
   A soft *Italian* lay,
Or where *Cam's* scanty waters flow,
   Releas'd from lectures, stray.
Meanwhile, friend BANKS, my merits claim
   Their just reward from you,
For HORACE bids us challenge fame,
   When once that fame's our due,
Invest me with a graduate's gown,

Midst shouts of all beholders,
My head with ample square-cap crown,
And deck with hood my shoulders.

Conviction

I like to get off with people,
I like to lie in their arms,
I like to be held and tightly kissed,
Safe from all alarms.

I like to laugh and be happy
With a beautiful beautiful kiss,
I tell you, in all the world
There is no bliss like this.

Sonnet (from *Amoretti*)

Oft when my spirit doth spread her bolder wings,
    In mind to mount up to the purest sky,
It down is weighed with thought of earthly things
    And clogged with burden of mortality,
    Where when that sovereign beauty it doth spy,
Resembling heaven's glory in her light,
    Drawn with sweet pleasure's bait, it back doth fly,
And unto heaven forgets her former flight.
There my frail fancy, fed with full delight,
    Doth bathe in bliss and mantleth most at ease:
Ne thinks of other heaven, but how it might
    Her heart's desire with most contentment please.
    Heart need not with none other happiness,
    But here on earth to have such heaven's bliss.

Poem in October

It was my thirtieth year to heaven
Woke to my hearing from harbour and neighbour wood
  And the mussel pooled and the heron
      Priested shore
    The morning beckon
With water praying and call of seagull and rook
And the knock of sailing boats on the net webbed wall
    Myself to set foot
      That second
In the still sleeping town and set forth.

My birthday began with the water-
Birds and the birds of the winged trees flying my name
  Above the farms and the white horses
      And I rose
    In rainy autumn
And walked abroad in a shower of all my days.
High tide and the heron dived when I took the road
    Over the border
      And the gates
Of the town closed as the town awoke.

A springful of larks in a rolling
Cloud and the roadside bushes brimming with whistling
  Blackbirds and the sun of October
      Summery
    On the hill's shoulder,
Here were fond climates and sweet singers suddenly
Come in the morning where I wandered and listened
    To the rain wringing

Wind blow cold
In the wood faraway under me.

Pale rain over the dwindling harbour
And over the sea wet church the size of a snail
With its horns through mist and the castle
Brown as owls
But all the gardens
Of spring and summer were blooming in the tall tales
Beyond the border and under the lark full cloud.
There could I marvel
My birthday
Away but the weather turned around.

It turned away from the blithe country
And down the other air and the blue altered sky
Streamed again a wonder of summer
With apples
Pears and red currants
And I saw in the turning so clearly a child's
Forgotten mornings when he walked with his mother
Through the parables
Of sun light
And the legends of the green chapels.

And the twice told fields of infancy
That his tears burned my cheeks and his heart moved in
mine
These were the woods the river and sea
Where a boy
In the listening
Summertime of the dead whispered the truth of his joy
To the trees and the stones and the fish in the tide.
And the mystery

    Sang alive
Still in the water and singingbirds.

  And there could I marvel my birthday
Away but the weather turned around. And the true
   Joy of the long dead child sang burning
      In the sun.
    It was my thirtieth
Year to heaven stood there then in the summer noon
Though the town below lay leaved with October blood.
   O may my heart's truth
     Still be sung
On this high hill in a year's turning.

Sowing

It was a perfect day
For sowing; just
As sweet and dry was the ground
As tobacco-dust.

I tasted deep the hour
Between the far
Owl's chuckling first soft cry
And the first star.

A long stretched hour it was;
Nothing undone
Remained; the early seeds
All safely sown.

And now, hark at the rain,
Windless and light,
Half a kiss, half a tear,
Saying good-night.

Tall Nettles

Tall nettles cover up, as they have done
These many springs, the rusty harrow, the plough
Long worn out, and the roller made of stone:
Only the elm butt tops the nettles now.

This corner of the farmyard I like most:
As well as any bloom upon a flower
I like the dust on the nettles, never lost
Except to prove the sweetness of a shower.

The Cobblers' Song

Trumpart	We cobblers lead a merry life,
All	Dan, dan, dan, dan;
Strumbo	Void of all envy and of strife,
All	Dan diddle dan.
Dorothy	Our ease is great, our labour small,
All	Dan, dan, dan, dan;
Strumbo	And yet our gains be much withal,
All	Dan diddle dan.
Dorothy	With this art so fine and fair,
All	Dan, dan, dan, dan,
Trumpart	No occupation may compare,
All	Dan diddle dan.
Strumbo	For merry pastime and joyful glee,
	Dan, dan, dan, dan,
Dorothy	Most happy men we cobblers be,
	Dan diddle dan.
Trumpart	The can stands full of nappy ale,
	Dan, dan, dan, dan;
Strumbo	In our shop still withouten fail,
	Dan diddle dan.
Dorothy	This is our meat, this is our food,
	Dan, dan, dan, dan;
Trumpart	This brings us to a merry mood,
	Dan diddle dan.
Strumbo	This makes us work for company,
	Dan, dan, dan, dan,
Dorothy	To pull the tankards cheerfully,
	Dan diddle dan.

Trumpart	Drink to thy husband, Dorothy,
	Dan, dan, dan, dan;
Dorothy	Why, then, my Strumbo, there's to thee,
	Dan diddle dan.
Strumbo	Drink thou the rest, Trumpart, amain,
	Dan, dan, dan, dan;
Dorothy	When that is gone, we'll fill 't again,
	Dan diddle dan.

The Salutation

These little limbs,
These eyes and hands which here I find,
These rosy cheeks wherewith my life begins,
Where have ye been? Behind
What curtain were ye from me hid so long?
Where was, in what abyss, my speaking tongue?

When silent I
So many thousand, thousand years,
Beneath the dust did in a chaos lie,
How could I smiles or tears,
Or lips or hands or eyes or ears perceive?
Welcome ye treasures which I now receive.

I that so long
Was nothing from eternity,
Did little think such joys as ear or tongue
To celebrate or see;
Such sounds to hear, such hands to feel, such feet,
Beneath the skies, on such a ground to meet.

New burnished joys!
Which yellow gold and pearl excel!
Such sacred treasures are the limbs in boys
In which a soul doth dwell:
Their organizèd joints and azure veins
More wealth include than all the world contains.

From dust I rise
And out of nothing now awake,
These brighter regions which salute mine eyes

A gift from God I take.
The earth, the seas, the light, the day, the skies,
The sun and stars are mine, if those I prize.

    Long time before
  I in my mother's womb was born,
A God preparing did this glorious store,
    The world, for me adorn.
Into this Eden so divine and fair,
So wide and bright, I come His son and heir.

    A stranger here
  Strange things doth meet, strange glories see;
Strange treasures lodged in this fair world appear,
    Strange all, and new to me.
But that they mine should be, who nothing was,
That strangest is of all, yet brought to pass.

In late-afternoon light the tops of the breadfruit leaves
are lemon and the lower leaves a waxen viridian
with the shaped shadows greenish black over the eaves
of the shops and the rust-crusted fences that are Indian
red, sepia, and often orange; but by then the light has
ripened and grass and the sides of the houses and even a
rooster crossing a yard blazes like a satrap; the lighthouse
is already on, and bulbs, and they are saying the novena
in the cathedral and the fishermen consciously become
silhouettes in the postcard sunset: this is when a
powerful smell of baked bread drifts and when the hum
of mosquitoes becomes tangible, when the road-ruts
deepen and faces that I love harder every year turn
towards the dusk and deepen also under the coconuts.
It is indigo now and the sea will continue to burn
until the last plane crosses with its green and red
wing-lights headed north and it is now definitely
night and the stars come where they were ordered
to protract the idea of patterns to infinity
and the sand exhales and there on the edge of the sea
green and red lights droning where stars and fireflies breed.

When I Heard at the Close of the Day

When I heard at the close of the day how my name had
    been receiv'd with plaudits in the capitol, still it was
    not a happy night for me that follow'd,
And else when I carous'd, or when my plans were
    accomplish'd, still I was not happy,But the day when I
rose at dawn from the bed of perfect
    health, refresh'd, singing, inhaling the ripe breath of
    autumn,
When I saw the full moon in the west grow pale and
    disappear in the morning light,
When I wander'd alone over the beach, and undressing
    bathed, laughing with the cool waters, and saw the sun
    rise,
And when I thought how my dear friend my lover was on
    his way coming, O then I was happy,
O then each breath tasted sweeter, and all that day my food
    nourish'd me more, and the beautiful day pass'd well,
And the next came with equal joy, and with the next at
    evening came my friend,
And that night while all was still I heard the waters roll
    slowly continually up the shores,
I heard the hissing rustle of the liquid and sands as
    directed to me whispering to congratulate me,
For the one I love most lay sleeping by me under the
    same cover in the cool night,
In the stillness in the autumn moonbeams his face was
    inclined toward me,
And his arm lay lightly around my breast – and that
    night I was happy.

April 5, 1974

The air was soft, the ground still cold.
In the dull pasture where I strolled
Was something I could not believe.
Dead grass appeared to slide and heave,
Though still too frozen-flat to stir,
And rocks to twitch, and all to blur.
What was this rippling of the land?
Was matter getting out of hand
And making free with natural law?
I stopped and blinked, and then I saw
A fact as eerie as a dream.
There was a subtle flood of steam
Moving upon the face of things.
It came from standing pools and springs
And what of snow was still around;
It came of winter's giving ground
So that the freeze was coming out,
As when a set mind, blessed by doubt,
Relaxes into mother-wit.
Flowers, I said, will come of it.

Iris

a burst of iris so that
come down for
breakfast

we searched through the
rooms for
that

sweetest odor and at
first could not
find its

source then a blue as
of the sea
struck

startling us from among
those trumpeting
petals

I wandered lonely as a cloud
That floats on high o'er vales and hills,
When all at once I saw a crowd,
A host, of golden daffodils;
Beside the lake, beneath the trees,
Fluttering and dancing in the breeze.

Continuous as the stars that shine
And twinkle on the milky way,
They stretched in never-ending line
Along the margin of a bay:
Ten thousand saw I at a glance,
Tossing their heads in sprightly dance.

The waves beside them danced; but they
Out-did the sparkling waves in glee:
A poet could not but be gay,
In such a jocund company:
I gazed – and gazed – but little thought
What wealth the show to me had brought:

For oft, when on my couch I lie
In vacant or in pensive mood,
They flash upon that inward eye
Which is the bliss of solitude;
And then my heart with pleasure fills,
And dances with the daffodils.

Composed upon Westminster Bridge

Earth has not anything to show more fair:
Dull would he be of soul who could pass by
A sight so touching in its majesty:
This City now doth, like a garment, wear
The beauty of the morning; silent, bare,
Ships, towers, domes, theatres, and temples lie
Open unto the fields, and to the sky;
All bright and glittering in the smokeless air.
Never did sun more beautifully steep
In his first splendour, valley, rock, or hill;
Ne'er saw I, never felt, a calm so deep!
The river glideth at his own sweet will:
Dear God! the very houses seem asleep;
And all that mighty heart is lying still!

Red Boots On

Way down Geneva,
All along Vine,
Deeper than the snow drift
Love's eyes shine:

Mary Lou's walking
In the winter time.

She's got

Red boots on, she's got
Red boots on,
Kicking up the winter
Till the winter's gone.

So

Go by Ontario,
Look down Main,
If you can't find Mary Lou,
Come back again:

Sweet light burning
In winter's flame.

She's got

Snow in her eyes, got
A tingle in her toes
And new red boots on
Wherever she goes.

So

All around Lake Street,
Up by St Paul,
Quicker than the white wind
Love takes all:

May Lou's walking
In the big snow fall.

She's got

Red boots on, she's got
Red boots on,
Kicking up the winter
Till the winter's gone.

Psalm 150

O praise God in his holiness: praise
him in the firmament of his power.

Praise him in his noble acts:
praise him according to his excellent greatness.

Praise him in the sound of the trumpet:
praise him upon the lute and harp.

Praise him in the cymbals and dances:
praise him upon the strings and pipe.

Praise him upon the well-tuned cymbals:
praise him upon the loud cymbals.

Let every thing that hath breath: praise the Lord.

Acknowledgements

The editor and publishers gratefully acknowledge permission to
reprint copyright material in this book as follows:

TACHIBANA AKEMI: 'Poems of Solitary Delights' from *The Penguin
Book of Japanese Verse*, translated by Bownas and Thwaite, published
by Penguin Books Ltd. FLEUR ADCOCK: 'Londoner' from *Poems
1960–2000*, published by Bloodaxe Books, 2000. SIMON
ARMITAGE: 'The Catch' from *Kid*, published by Faber and Faber Ltd,
reproduced by permission of the publisher. W. H. AUDEN: 'Calypso'
from *W. H. Auden: Collected Poems*, copyright © 1976 by Edward
Mendelson, William Meredith and Monroe K. Spears, Executors of
the Estate of W. H. Auden, used by permission of Random House Inc
and Faber and Faber Ltd. CONNIE BENSLEY: 'Soothsayer' from
Choosing to be a Swan, published by Bloodaxe Books, 1994. JOHN
BETJEMAN: 'Seaside Golf' from *Collected Poems*, reproduced by
permission of John Murray Publishers Ltd. NINA CASSIAN:
'Intimacy', translated by Eva Feiler and Nina Cassian, from *Life
Sentence: Selected Poems*, edited by William J. Smith, published by
Anvil Press Poetry, 1990. JOHN CLARE: 'The Hollow Tree' and
'Sabbath Bells' from *Selected Poems and Prose of John Clare*, edited by
Eric Robinson and Geoffrey Summerfield, reproduced with
permission of Curtis Brown Group Ltd, London of behalf of Eric
Robinson, copyright © Eric Robinson, 1966. E. E. CUMMINGS: 'i
thank You God for this most amazing' from *Complete Poems 1904-
1962*, edited by George J. Firmage, by permission of W. W. Norton &
Co., copyright © 1991 by the Trustees for the E. E. Cummings Trust
and George James Firmage. DICK DAVIS: 'Uxor Vivamus' from *Devices
and Desires: New and Selected Poems 1967-1987*, published by Anvil
Press Poetry, 1989. EMILY DICKINSON: 'A soft sea washed around
the House' and 'I taste a liquor never brewed', reprinted by
permission of the publishers and the Trustees of Amherst College
from *The Poems of Emily Dickinson*, Thomas H. Johnson, ed.,
Cambridge, Mass.: The Belknap Press of Harvard University Press,
copyright © 1951, 1955, 1979 by the President and Fellows of

Harvard College. MICHAEL DONAGHY: 'Held' from *Dances Learned Last Night*, reproduced by permission of Picador. MAURA DOOLEY: 'Up on the Roof' from *Kissing a Bone*, published by Bloodaxe Books, 1996. CAROL ANN DUFFY: 'A Child's Sleep' from *Meeting Midnight*, published by Faber and Faber Ltd, reproduced by permission of the publisher. HELEN DUNMORE: 'Privacy of Rain' from *Short Days, Long Nights: New and Selected Poems*, published by Bloodaxe Books, 1991. PAUL DURCAN: '10.30 a.m. Mass, June 16, 1985' reprinted by kind permission of the author. D. J. ENRIGHT: 'And Two Good Things' from *Collected Poems*, published by Oxford University Press, reproduced by permission of Watson Little Ltd. GAVIN EWART: 'June 1996' from *The Collected Ewart 1933-1980*, published by Hutchinson, reproduced by kind permission of Margot Ewart. U. A. FANTHORPE: '7301', copyright © U. A. Fanthorpe from *A Watching Brief*, published by Peterloo Poets, 1987, reproduced by permission of the publisher. ELEANOR FARJEON: 'Morning has broken' from *The Children's Bells*, published by Oxford University Press, reproduced by permission of David Higham Associates Ltd. ELAINE FEINSTEIN: 'Getting Older' from *Selected Poems*, reproduced by permission of Carcanet Press Ltd. ROBERT FROST: 'Mowing' from *The Poetry of Robert Frost*, edited by Edward Connery Lathem, the Estate of Robert Frost and Jonathan Cape as publisher, used by permission of The Random House Group Ltd; copyright © 1962 by Robert Frost, copyright © 1934, 1969 by Henry Holt and Co.; reprinted in Canada by permission of Henry Holt and Company LLC. ROBERT GRAVES: 'Song: The Palm Tree' from *Collected Poems*, reproduced by permission of Carcanet Press Ltd. THOM GUNN: 'Sweet Things' from *Collected Poems*, published by Faber and Faber Ltd, reproduced by permission of the publisher. TED HUGHES: 'Full Moon and Little Frieda' from *Wodwo*, published by Faber and Faber Ltd, reproduced by permission of the publisher. PHILIP LARKIN: 'For Sidney Bechet' from *Whitsun Weddings*, published by Faber and Faber Ltd, reproduced by permission of the publisher. NORMAN MACCAIG: 'Small Rain' and 'Ballade of Good Whiskey' from *Collected Poems*, published by Hogarth Press, reproduced by permission of The Random House Group Limited. EDWIN MORGAN: 'One Cigarette' from *Collected Poems*, reproduced by permission of Carcanet Press Ltd. ANDREW MOTION: 'You Do, I Do' from *Natural Causes*, reproduced by permission of Peters Fraser & Dunlop Group Limited. EDWIN MUIR: 'The Confirmation' from *Collected Poems*, published by

Faber and Faber Ltd, reproduced by permission of the publisher.
SYLVIA PLATH: 'You're' from *Ariel*, published by Faber and Faber
Ltd, reproduced by permission of the publisher. CRAIG RAINE:
'Heaven on Earth' from *Clay, Whereabouts Unknown*, reproduced by
permission of David Godwin Associates. CHRISTOPHER REID: 'The
South' from *Katerina Brac*, published by Faber and Faber Ltd,
reproduced by permission of the publisher. ŌSHIMA RYŌTA: 'Bad-
tempered, I got back' from *The Penguin Book of Japanese Verse*,
translated by Bownas and Thwaite, published by Penguin Books Ltd.
SEIGFRIED SASSOON: 'Everyone Sang', copyright © Seigfried
Sassoon, reproduced by kind permission of George Sassoon.
PENELOPE SHUTTLE: 'Delicious Babies' from *Selected Poems*,
reproduced by permission of Carcanet Press Ltd. STEVIE SMITH:
'Conviction', reproduced by permission of the Estate of James
McGibbon. DYLAN THOMAS:'Poem in October' from *Collected Poems*,
published by J. M. Dent, reproduced by permission of David Higham
Associates Ltd. DEREK WALCOTT: 'In late-afternoon light . . .' from
The Bounty, published by Faber and Faber Ltd, reproduced by
permission of the publisher. WILLIAM CARLOS WILLIAMS: 'Iris'
from *Collected Poems, Volume II*, reproduced by permission of
Carcanet Press Ltd. KIT WRIGHT: 'Red Boots On', reproduced by kind
permission of the author.

Index of Poets

Index of First Lines